THE
WEARY
WORLD
REJOICES

DAILY DEVOTIONS
for ADVENT

CONTENTS

TGC
ADVENT
DEVOTIONAL

For generations, churches and families have used Advent wreaths to help prepare their hearts and minds for celebrating the Lord's birth at Christmas. The evergreen wreath symbolizes eternal life and includes four candles, typically three purple and one pink. Often, there is a white candle in the middle of the wreath symbolizing the purity of Christ. Various traditions assign different topics to each individual candle, and the candles are usually given names to remind us of the good news of Christ's birth.

To celebrate this season, TGC's editorial team has put together these devotional readings that use the Advent wreath as a guide to help focus our hearts and minds on Christ during the month of December. We've chosen the following themes to accompany each of the five weeks:

- WEEK 1 (HOPE)
  Prophecy Candle (John 1:45)

- WEEK 2 (PEACE)
  Bethlehem Candle (Mic. 5:2; Isa. 9:6)

- WEEK 3 (JOY)
  Shepherd Candle (Luke 2:20; Isa. 35:10)

- WEEK 4 (LOVE)
  Angel Candle (Luke 2:13–14; John 3:16)

- WEEK 5 (FAITH)
  Christ Candle (John 1:29; Eph. 2:8–10)

HOW TO USE THIS GUIDE

This book offers 25 devotions, with each day providing a Bible reading, devotional reflection, questions for response, and a hymn stanza for rejoicing. You can begin the devotional on December 1 and have one reading per day until Christmas. Or, if you prefer to follow the Sundays in Advent, you can use these reflections for five days a week leading up to Christmas, and then use the final week after Christmas (week 5) to continue to reflect on a life of faith in light of the good news of Christ's birth.

If you'd like to use this guide with your family, you could pick one devotion from each week to accompany the lighting of your Advent wreath in the home. In whatever ways you choose to use this devotional, we hope and pray that these readings will encourage your heart and help your mind focus on Jesus throughout this season.

We celebrate the good news proclaimed by Isaiah so long ago:

For to us a child is born,
    to us a son is given;
and the government shall be upon his shoulder,
    and his name shall be called
Wonderful Counselor, Mighty God,
    Everlasting Father, Prince of Peace. (Isa. 9:6)

Rejoicing with you,
Melissa Kruger

Philip found Nathanael and said to him, "We have found him of whom Moses in the Law and also the prophets wrote, Jesus of Nazareth, the son of Joseph."

JOHN 1:45

HOPE

Prophecy Candle

DAY 1

A HOPEFUL COMPANY

Megan Hill

READ

"And there was a prophetess, Anna, the daughter of Phanuel, of the tribe of Asher. She was advanced in years, having lived with her husband seven years from when she was a virgin, and then as a widow until she was eighty-four. She did not depart from the temple, worshiping with fasting and prayer night and day. And coming up at that very hour she began to give thanks to God and to speak of him to all who were waiting for the redemption of Jerusalem." (Luke 2:36–38)

REFLECT

So much of the Christmas bustle seems to miss the point. Our neighbors focus on traditions or togetherness but fail to seek the baby in the manger. Our co-workers and friends delight in "the season" but overlook the hope of all the earth. Even our own family members are often more concerned about their stocking stuffers than about the desperate need of their undying souls. To truly celebrate Christmas, we need better company.

Today's verses introduce us to the prophetess Anna and her faithful companions; Scripture tells us they were "waiting for the redemption of Jerusalem." In contrast to many of their fellow Jews, this band of believers maintained their hope in the coming Messiah. Despite hundreds of years of prophetic silence, they committed themselves to worship and prayer in the temple, and they looked eagerly for the One who would "redeem Israel from all his iniquities" (Ps. 130:8). While the people around them were chasing the fading things of earth or superficially practicing outward religion, these friends had set their hearts on Christ.

Now, as then, God's people often seek him in the dark. We live many years after Christ's first appearing, and we may begin to grow weary of waiting for his return. The difficulties of life in a fallen world weigh heavily on us, and we are sometimes hard-pressed to remain hopeful. What's more, the world, the flesh, and the Evil One continually hold out glittering objects to catch the eyes of our heart. "Forget about eternity," they whisper. "This is now."

Thankfully, we don't have to persevere alone. God has surrounded us with a hopeful company: his beloved church. By their example and exhortation, the members of our local churches become a cloud of witnesses pointing to Jesus. As we read God's Word together, we grow in our knowledge of the Redeemer. As we sing songs of praise, our hearts are lifted to the One who is worthy. As we share stories of God's grace, we look for the Spirit's work in the unseen places of our own hearts. Week after week, our fellow believers testify that this world is not all there is, and they remind us that the people of God have always lived for another world entirely. In the company of the church, we focus on Christ.

Anna and her friends received the reward for their patient endurance. Having devoted themselves to being in the place of God's presence, they were there "at that very hour" (v. 38) when the Savior of the world appeared. Like those first-century believers, we also should commit ourselves to hoping in Christ and worshiping him together. And as we do, we will be in the very best place to experience his presence. "For where two or three are gathered in my name," Jesus promises, "there am I among them" (Matt. 18:20). In the company of the hopeful, Christ makes himself known.

RESPOND

Why do you sometimes struggle to remain hopeful? How does the fellowship of other believers encourage you to hope in Christ? Where do you have opportunities to speak words of hope to those around you?

REJOICE

To us a child of hope is born, to us a son is giv'n,
Him shall the tribes of earth obey, him all the hosts of heaven

–John Morison, "To Us a Child of Hope is Born"

DAY 2

HOPE FULFILLED

Winfree Brisley

READ

"Philip found Nathanael and said to him, 'We have found him of whom Moses in the Law and also the prophets wrote, Jesus of Nazareth, the son of Joseph.'" (John 1:45)

REFLECT

One of our favorite family stories is about the time my husband's cousin made a particularly ambitious Christmas list. He copied down practically every item from a thick toy catalogue. Then, he added one final request: surprises.

Many of us go to great lengths to pull off a Christmas morning surprise. Even now, you may have gifts hidden away, tucked into nooks and crannies, or delivered to a neighbor's house for safekeeping. Perhaps you've hunted down a gift that's nearly impossible to secure. Maybe you'll be up late on Christmas Eve doing a last-minute assembly.

Surprises can be delightful to give and receive, creating a sense of wonder and excitement around Christmas. But as we enjoy them, it's good to remember that the advent of Christ wasn't meant to be a surprise. God had been promising his people a serpent-crushing offspring from the earliest pages of the Bible (Gen. 3:15). The real story of Christmas is not a story of surprise but of fulfillment.

Through the Old Testament prophets, God revealed quite a bit of information about the coming Messiah. Jeremiah said he would be a king from the line of David (Jer. 23:5–6). Micah foretold he would come from the town of Bethlehem (Mic. 5:2). Isaiah said he would be born of a virgin (Isa. 7:14). Years ahead of time, God promised his people a Savior and gave specific details about his coming.

So, when Philip went to share the news that Christ had come, notice what he said: "We have found him of whom Moses . . . and also the prophets wrote" (John 1:45). He didn't say, "Surprise! God sent a Savior." He said, "We have *found* him." They knew the Messiah was coming. They were expecting him. Finding Jesus, for them, was confirmation of God's faithfulness.

And that's the story of Christmas for us, too. The advent of Christ is a vivid reminder that God does what he says he will do, down to the last detail. Don't skip over the details the Gospel writers record about the birth of Christ. It's not extra fluff to fill out the story. In Matthew's account of Christ's birth, five times he writes something like, "This was to fulfill what the Lord had spoken by the prophet" (see Matt. 1:22; 2:5, 15, 17, 23). Why does Matthew repeatedly point out the fulfillment of prophecy? Because it shows us God's faithfulness.

God's faithfulness in the Christmas story gives us hope in our own stories. Just as God promised to send Jesus, he promises to be with us now through the indwelling presence of the Holy Spirit. Just as Jesus came the first time, he promises to come again. We can look forward in hope, confidently anticipating Christ's second coming and the fulfillment of his promises to dwell with us forever (Rev. 21:3).

God may not give us everything on our wish list, but we can be sure he will fulfill all of the promises he has made. Great is his faithfulness!

RESPOND

How have you seen God's faithfulness to you in the past? In what areas of your life are you struggling to believe God's promises? What might it look like for you to find hope in God's faithfulness today?

REJOICE

Pardon for sin and a peace that endureth,
Thine own dear presence to cheer and to guide;
Strength for today and bright hope for tomorrow,
Blessings all mine, with ten thousand beside!
Great is Thy faithfulness!

-Thomas Chisholm, "Great Is Thy Faithfulness"

DAY 3

HOPE IN SCORCHED PLACES

Melissa Kruger

READ

"And the LORD will guide you continually and satisfy your desire in scorched places and make your bones strong; and you shall be like a watered garden, like a spring of water, whose waters do not fail." (Isa. 58:11)

REFLECT

We often assume the Lord only leads us to green pastures, settling us beside still waters. While a peaceful place of rest is certainly his ultimate destination, at times we travel through scorched places, where fiery trials and destructive storms threaten to overwhelm and consume (Isa. 43:2). These times of testing and trials are uniquely painful and can feel all the more difficult during the Christmas season. Only the Lord can continually walk with us, strengthen us, and meet us with his unfailing compassion.

Thankfully, he meets our powerlessness with the promise of his presence: "I will be with you" (Isa. 43:2). At the incarnation, the fulfillment of this promise was on display for the world to see: God became man and dwelt among us. Though the path may be unclear and the way precarious, we have the One who can lead us. We cannot know the way or the why, but we know the One we follow.

We tend to believe contentment blooms once we've reached those much-longed-for green pastures. However, this passage directs us to a different promise of blessing: God satisfies our desire *within* the scorched places, reminding us that perfect circumstances cannot fulfill our desires—only he can. Jesus awakens joy—enough to make scorched places brim with satisfaction (Ps. 16:11). He meets our deepest longings by removing outward comforts so we may drink more deeply of our ultimate comfort.

God strengthens us within the suffering, not by removing the trial but by being an ever-present help within it. Perhaps sleepless nights, difficult conversations, and unexpected waves of grief have left you weary and worn. You may feel like you have nothing to offer. At times, he leads us through scorched places just so we have nothing else to rely on but himself. When the landscape is barren, we must cry to him for bread. And, mercy of mercies, he does not leave us hungry. His Word is a feast that imbues strength in the struggle so we may bear all things, hope all things, and endure all things. We sing with the psalmist, "This is my comfort in my affliction, that your promise gives me life" (Ps. 119:50).

Perhaps the most significant surprise comes at the end of this passage: "You shall be like a watered garden, like a spring of water, whose waters do not fail" (Isa. 58:11). In our scorched places, we don't just survive—God makes us a spring that overflows. Not only are we refreshed, but he allows us opportunities to refresh others. During this season of Advent, we have opportunity to share the hope that's with us. In the midst of our scorched places, he alone satisfies, strengthens, and refreshes us.

RESPOND

What places in your life seem scorched and barren? In what ways does the promise of God's presence and power amid these trials give you hope today?

REJOICE

A thrill of hope, the weary world rejoices
For yonder breaks a new and glorious morn'
Fall on your knees, oh, hear the Angels' voices
Oh, night divine, oh, night when Christ was born
Oh, night divine, oh, night, oh night divine

–Placide Cappeau, "O Holy Night"

DAY 4

HOPE AND FEAR

Courtney Doctor

READ

"But you, O Bethlehem Ephrathah, who are too little to be among the clans of Judah, from you shall come forth for me one who is to be ruler in Israel, whose coming forth is from of old, from ancient days." (Mic. 5:2)

REFLECT

I've been to Bethlehem. The town itself is unremarkable. One of the most memorable parts of my visit was a coffee shop by the name of Stars & Bucks. The sign was a green and white circle with a very familiar font.

Of course, people don't flock by the millions each year to see a knock-off coffee shop. They go to see the Church of the Nativity—the site believed to be the birthplace of Jesus. Today's verse comes to us from the prophet Micah, who prophesied approximately 700 years before Jesus made his entrance in Bethlehem.

Micah calls the town "too little to be among the clans of Judah"—Bethlehem was such a small, obscure, and overlooked village, it was hardly worth counting. It was an unlikely location for great things to happen. But our God specializes in taking the unlikely, obscure, and overlooked, and doing great things: "From you shall come forth for me one who is to be ruler in Israel." A king. The Messiah. From Bethlehem.

Centuries before Micah penned his prophecy, another unlikely king came from Bethlehem. David, the shepherd boy who became the mighty warrior and great king, was born in this obscure town. David was the most unlikely of his brothers. Samuel almost overlooked him. Yet David was the Lord's choice (1 Sam. 16). He became the greatest king Israel had ever had, a man after God's own heart (1 Sam. 13:14).

Israel waited and longed for another king like David, a good and righteous ruler. But, as the years went by, they feared the Lord had forgotten them.

Waiting. Hope. Fear. They go hand-in-hand. We fear our hopes won't be realized, the waiting will never end, or the answer won't be to our liking. We fear we've been forgotten or overlooked, too obscure to be of any importance.

But, because of what happened on a still night in a remote village, you and I never have to fear again. Our truest hope and deepest longing collided with our greatest fear—not just in Bethlehem, but in Jesus.

Waiting is still hard. Hope deferred can cause us to doubt. But because of what happened in Bethlehem, we wait with confidence. The God who sent his Son into an obscure and unlikely town to fulfill all hope is the same God who still draws near to everyone who feels overlooked. We haven't been forgotten—we've been redeemed.

We don't sing about this small village because it was great. We sing because greatness itself chose to come to us in this unlikely place. So, anchor all your hopes, all your longings, all your waiting, and all your fears in Jesus.

"And now, O Lord, for what do I wait? My hope is in you" (Ps. 39:7).

RESPOND

What are you waiting on or fearful about today? In what ways does this story remind you that you are not overlooked or forgotten by God?

REJOICE

O little town of Bethlehem, how still we see thee lie
Above thy deep and dreamless sleep the silent stars go by
Yet in thy dark streets shineth, the everlasting light
The hopes and fears of all the years are met in thee tonight.

–Phillips Brooks, "O Little Town of Bethlehem"

DAY 5

SIGH NO MORE

Brett McCracken

READ

"And the ransomed of the LORD shall return and come to Zion with singing; everlasting joy shall be upon their heads; they shall obtain gladness and joy, and sorrow and sighing shall flee away." (Isa. 35:10)

REFLECT

The essence of hope is not the downplaying, justifying, or avoidance of present pain and sorrow. Rather, hope is the expectation that as real as the pain is now, it will one day feel as foreign as our faintest memories.

In our day, we can relate to the experience of "ransom captive Israel," who mourned "in lonely exile here, until the Son of God appear." As Israel waited—in bondage to suffering, sin, pain, and injustice—so we wait now. Sorrow is everywhere: in the bleak headlines that cross our feeds, in the sickness and death that plague our own friends and family, and in the temptation and sin that leave us feeling frustrated, defeated, even hopeless.

Sighing is everywhere too. We sigh at the exhausting pace of life and the busy schedules we can never seem to simplify. We sigh at the foolishness we see all around us (perhaps particularly on social media). We sigh at the sin that creeps in and wreaks havoc everywhere: in our relationships, in our churches, in the divisions between Christians that grow uglier every day.

But one day our sighing will turn to singing. Our sorrow will turn to gladness and joy—*everlasting* joy. The words of Isaiah 35:10 are words of healing and hope: "sorrow and sighing shall flee away." I can't wait for that day. It can't come soon enough. But as we live in the "now" before that "not yet" day, we hope. We long. We wait. And the tension of waiting can be beautiful.

I love the Mumford and Sons album, *Sigh No More* (2010). The title is a reference to a line in Shakespeare's *Much Ado About Nothing*, but the whole album—which is littered with biblical and theological references—captures the beautiful longing that the title suggests. Perhaps you can look the album up on your favorite streaming music service during Advent and give it a listen. It's not Christmas music, but to the extent that it expresses the human hope for a world where "sighing shall flee away," it captures some of Advent's themes.

One day, indeed, we will sigh no more. Will we forget what sorrow was like? I'm not sure. Perhaps in eternity, in that "everlasting joy" presence of God, we'll actually laugh and reminisce and tell tales of old—remembering those days on Earth when things like sorrow and sighing were *things*. Maybe it'll be similar to those holiday family gatherings where we nostalgically look through scrapbooks or pull out dusty mementos from long forgotten times. Why? Not because we want to return to or relive that past. But because it was real. The ups and downs. The struggles and sorrows. The fits and starts of joy.

Maybe one day—when "Emmanuel" is our everyday experience (hallelujah!)—we'll look back on this life of lonely exile and feel gratitude for how the sighs and sorrows made us hungrier for the everlasting feast, and the fullness of joy, that will be ours forever.

RESPOND

What "sighs" are you experiencing now in your life? Take these honestly to the Lord in prayer. Physically sigh as you think about them. Then spend time reflecting on the future described in Isaiah 35:10, when "sorrow and sighing shall flee away." Dream about that day.

REJOICE

O come, O come, Emmanuel,
and ransom captive Israel
that mourns in lonely exile here
until the Son of God appear.

–Author unknown (Tr. by John Mason Neale),
"O Come, O Come, Emmanuel"

But you, O Bethlehem Ephrathah,
who are too little to be among the clans of Judah,
from you shall come forth for me
one who is to be ruler in Israel,
whose coming forth is from of old,
from ancient days.

MICAH 5:2

For to us a child is born,
to us a son is given;
and the government shall be upon his shoulder,
and his name shall be called
Wonderful Counselor, Mighty God,
Everlasting Father, Prince of Peace.

ISAIAH 9:6

PEACE

Bethlehem Candle

DAY 6

WHERE PEACE
IS FOUND

Matt Smethurst

READ

"For to us a child is born, to us a son is given; and the government shall be upon his shoulder, and his name shall be called Wonderful Counselor, Mighty God, Everlasting Father, Prince of Peace. Of the increase of his government and of peace there will be no end, on the throne of David and over his kingdom, to establish it and to uphold it with justice and with righteousness from this time forth and forevermore. The zeal of the LORD of hosts will do this." (Isa. 9:6–7)

REFLECT

Peace, as an idea, is immensely popular. We love talking about it, posting about it, dreaming about it, planning for it.

But it sure can be elusive, can't it?

Despite its universally beloved status, peace does not mark our world—and I don't simply mean unsettling headlines from distant lands. Peace eludes those in the securest neighborhoods, the richest professions, the most advanced nations. Peace eludes us even when we've arrived.

In his 2009 NBA Hall of Fame speech, Michael Jordan called the game of basketball his "refuge," the "place where I've gone when I needed to find comfort and peace." A few years later, on the occasion of his 50th birthday, the restlessness remained. In a candid interview with ESPN's Wright Thompson, Jordan pondered aloud: "How can I enjoy the next 20 years without so much of this consuming me? How can I find peace away from the game of basketball?"[1]

The answer, it turns out—both for Jordan and for us—is found in an ancient scroll.

Seven centuries before the Messiah's birth, Isaiah the prophet issued a divine forecast. Addressing the Israelites, who were about to be exiled for their rebellion and idolatry, he pointed them to a future time when a solution—an undeserved remedy—would descend from God himself. He even hinted that the remedy would *be* God himself.

This coming gift is cosmic in proportion and yet also intensely personal. Notice the recipient: "to us" (v. 6). Israel's name is on the label. And the contents are divine: the promised child will be none less than the "Mighty God."

Moreover, it's a gift tied to the very thing that eludes us. The promised child will also be called the "Prince of Peace"—a fitting title because, for his people, there will be no end to "the increase of his government and of peace." No exceptions, no elusiveness, no expiration date.

1.   Wright Thompson, "Michael Jordan Has Not Left the Building." Available at http://www.espn.com/espn/feature/story/_/page/Michael-Jordan/michael-jordan-not-left-building.

And the reason this promise will hold is because the gospel is bigger than a nativity scene. The incarnation of Jesus Christ was an invasion, both a dawning of peace and a declaration of war. The baby in the manger didn't stay there, after all—he grew up and obeyed his Father to the point of death, even death on a cross. Suspended on Roman wood, he made peace between God and man (Eph. 2:14-17).

No other religion teaches anything like this. Each one insists, in some form or another, that *you* must achieve the peace of God, some semblance of transcendental tranquility—which is also why it never happens. How could it? As a sinner you are the problem in this equation, not the solution. In Christianity, however, you can:

receive the peace of God, through trusting Jesus;
enjoy the peace of God, through following Jesus;
spread the peace of God, through proclaiming Jesus.

Friend, if you want to experience the peace of God, you must know the God of peace. And if you want to know the God of peace, you must embrace his only begotten Son.

Real peace is not found in a basketball arena or a Hall of Fame ceremony. It's not found in a successful job or a secure neighborhood. It's not found in food or exercise or travel or holiday cheer. It's not even found in a loving family or a vibrant ministry. In the final analysis, peace is only found in the Prince of it.

RESPOND

In what created thing has your heart been seeking peace? How might the gospel of grace liberate you from that exhausting pursuit—reordering your loves and redirecting your allegiance to the Prince of Peace?

REJOICE

Hail the heaven-born Prince of Peace!
Hail the Sun of righteousness!
Light and life to all he brings,
Risen with healing in his wings.

–Charles Wesley, "Hark! The Herald Angels Sing"

DAY 7

PEACE
IS JUSTICE

Collin Hansen

READ

"And Mary said, 'My soul magnifies the Lord, and my spirit rejoices in God my Savior, for he has looked on the humble estate of his servant. For behold, from now on all generations will call me blessed; for he who is mighty has done great things for me, and holy is his name. And his mercy is for those who fear him from generation to generation. He has shown strength with his arm; he has scattered the proud in the thoughts of their hearts; he has brought down the mighty from their thrones and exalted those of humble estate; he has filled the hungry with good things, and the rich he has sent away empty. He has helped his servant Israel, in remembrance of his mercy, as he spoke to our fathers, to Abraham and to his offspring forever.'" (Luke 1:46–55)

REFLECT

Sometimes I wonder if the real Mary will ever break out of the ancient paintings that domesticated her. Every time I roll past Luke 1 in my Bible reading, I'm struck again by her extraordinary prayer, worthy of the Old Testament prophets. Two thousand years later, our generation calls her blessed. She carried in her womb her very Savior—and ours.

Mary, anticipating the peace that would follow great upheaval, rejoices in the promises of God. Her world, and ours, is filled with injustice. The proud seem to prosper. The mighty take advantage of the weak. The humble get trampled. The hungry wither away. A woman with no husband, carrying a child, Mary was vulnerable, easily exploited.

But Mary sees the world through the eyes of faith. The Lord has looked on her with favor. He has chosen her for an extraordinary task. The promise is almost too wonderful to imagine. Through her child, conceived of the Holy Spirit, all oppression one day would cease. Her people—the offspring of Abraham, and all of us who would believe Jesus by faith—would hunger and thirst for righteousness no longer. They would be satisfied in peace, because Jesus would satisfy the justice of his Father through death on the cross.

Mary offered herself as the servant of God by carrying the Christ. And her son would fulfill the hopes of Israel as the Suffering Servant foretold by the prophet Isaiah. He would be pierced, because we sinned. He would be crushed, because we committed iniquity. Because he would be chastised, we would know peace. Because he would be wounded, we would be healed.

This is the future Mary saw—when peace would come through justice. The child she carried would grow up and put an end to death's hold on us. No longer would sin consign us to punishment, as we deserved. And when Jesus comes again, he will put an end to sin altogether. He will bring everlasting peace through his final judgment. The mighty will be humbled. The rich will be denuded.

But God will spare everyone who fears him. The Father remembered mercy when he entrusted his only Son to this daughter of Israel. When Jesus returns, we'll love one another in perfect righteousness. All oppression will cease. Mary knew her baby boy would save many sons and daughters—generation after generation of the faithful.

RESPOND

How does the expectation of future justice help you to fight against injustice today? Where can you bring love today to a world that remains in bondage to oppression?

REJOICE

Truly he taught us to love one another
His law is love and his gospel is peace
Chains shall he break for the slave is our brother
And in his name all oppression shall cease

–Placide Cappeau, "O Holy Night"

DAY 8

PEACE IN
THE LONELINESS

Quina Aragon

READ

"Turn to me and be gracious to me, for I am lonely and afflicted. The troubles of my heart are enlarged; bring me out of my distresses. Consider my affliction and my trouble, and forgive all my sins. Consider how many are my foes, and with what violent hatred they hate me. Oh, guard my soul, and deliver me! Let me not be put to shame, for I take refuge in you." (Ps. 25:16–20)

REFLECT

Two Decembers ago, my husband and I celebrated Christmas with Colombian food (his side of the family), Filipino traditions (my side of the family), and the sting of death. Tragedies had cascaded one-by-one throughout that year until our running joke was, "Good morning. What's our emergency today?" Little did we know, the infamous 2020 was right around the corner.

Through 2020 and 2021 we've likely all been touched by the sting of death—the death of family members or friends, the death of dreams, or perhaps the death of community life. If there's one Bible verse we've surely resonated with, it's this: "I am lonely and afflicted" (v. 16). And loneliness is often heightened during the Christmas season.

Loneliness is a form of suffering. But it's just the sort of thing we tend to shy away from admitting. We might even confuse it for sin itself: *How can I feel lonely if God is always with me? I must not be trusting him very well.* Of course, loneliness is a byproduct of mankind's rebellion (Gen. 3), but loneliness itself isn't sin. And it's not insignificant to God.

King David prayed God would turn to him with grace in his loneliness. He knew the lack of peace brought on by his own sins *and* the sins of others against him. He cried, "Consider my affliction and my trouble, and forgive all my sins" (v. 18). We know what that feels like. The compounded grief we carry becomes (so we think) license to snap at our loved ones or to escape with the fleeting pleasures of sexual sin. We're left feeling estranged from God and others, longing for peace.

But David also cried, "Consider how many are my foes, and with what violent hatred they hate me" (v. 19). Essentially, "I've sinned *and* I've been sinned against. And they both hurt." They both threaten our experience of peace (wholeness) with God and others. We're left fractured.

But the greater son of David, the Lord Jesus Christ, was coming. His cries would break through a lonely night in Bethlehem as he wriggled in a feeding trough. His cries would break through a lonely night in the Garden of Gethsemane as he writhed before the prospect of the cross. His cries would break through the midday darkness as he suffered ul-

timate loneliness—separation from God's loving presence—
when he paid for our sins.

His coming meant the securing of eternal peace between
you and God, and you and others—the death of loneliness.

RESPOND

Pray these verses from Psalm 25 back to God, interjecting
the particular troubles you face today. Trust that God hears,
cares, and draws near to you in your pain.

REJOICE

Comfort, comfort, O my people,
speak of peace, now says our God.
Comfort those who sit in shadows,
mourning 'neath their sorrows' load.
Speak unto Jerusalem
of the peace that waits for them.
Tell of all the sins I cover,
and that warfare now is over.

–Johann Olearius (Tr. by Catherine Winkworth),
"Comfort, Comfort Ye My People"

PEACE ON EARTH

Justin Dillehay

READ

"'And this will be a sign for you: you will find a baby wrapped in swaddling cloths and lying in a manger.' And suddenly there was with the angel a multitude of the heavenly host praising God and saying, 'Glory to God in the highest, and on earth peace among those with whom he is pleased!'" (Luke 2:12–14)

REFLECT

Between 1912 and 1917, Europe was decimated by the worst war in human history. So horrific was it that people wistfully referred to it as "the war to end all wars." Little did they know that, within a few decades, this period of carnage would have to be renamed "World War I" to distinguish it from an even bloodier conflict.

Ever since sin entered the world, peace has been fleeting. Indeed, fallen men are so prone to violence that a righteous sword is required to restrain them (Rom. 13:1–7). And yet our hearts yearn for paradise lost, where the lion ate straw like an ox and there was nothing to hurt or destroy in all God's holy mountain (Isa. 65:25; cf. Gen. 1:30). Thankfully, God's prophets have promised us that a new and better Eden is coming, where "nation shall not lift up sword against nation, neither shall they learn war anymore" (Isa. 2:4; Mic. 4:3; cf. Isa. 11:6–9).

A quick glance at the newspaper should convince us that this prophecy belongs to the "not yet" aspect of the kingdom. And yet meditating on passages like Luke 2:14 should also convince us that God is already restoring peace to the earth in some measure. There is a group of people "with whom [God] is pleased," among whom true shalom exists. We call them the church—all those who by faith have embraced the "Prince of Peace" as their Savior (Isa. 9:6).

As those justified by faith, we now have peace with God (Rom. 5:1). Our reconciliation to God reconciles us to each other—Christ has "broken down in his flesh the dividing wall of hostility . . . that he might create in himself one new man . . . so making peace" (Eph. 2:14, 16). His peace toward us allows us to extend peace to others.

This doesn't make peace automatic or easy. If it did, many of the exhortations in Paul's epistles would never have been written. But it's who we are. Our task as Christians is to increasingly become like Christ, to walk worthy of our calling, and to maintain the unity of the Spirit in the bond of peace (Eph. 4:3). By the Spirit, we pursue peace with our enemies and make war on the passions that cause quarrels among us (Gal. 5:16; James 4:1).

However, the "war to end all wars" has already been fought. It was launched on Christmas, won on Good Friday, and proclaimed on Easter morning. And though it awaits its full consummation, we see tiny previews of it every time we forgive one another, or baptize a new convert, or commune around the Lord's Table. May these glimpses of his grace awaken our hearts in praise: "Glory to God in the highest, and on earth peace among those with whom he is pleased!" (v. 14).

RESPOND

In what practical ways can you seek to maintain peace among the Christians in your local church? Does peace characterize your life online in the way you relate to others?

REJOICE

Hark! the herald angels sing
"Glory to the newborn King
Peace on earth and mercy mild,
God and sinners reconciled!"

–Charles Wesley, "Hark! The Herald Angels Sing"

DAY 10

NOT ENOUGH TIME

Sarah Eekhoff Zylstra

READ

"Peace I leave with you; my peace I give to you. Not as the world gives do I give to you. Let not your hearts be troubled, neither let them be afraid." (John 14:27)

REFLECT

"You hate Christmas," my husband told me last year.

"I don't either!"

"You do."

We were both right. I love Christmas—but I kind of hate it, too. Not because of the gifts or the concerts or the parties—I love those things. I love the lights, the hot chocolate, and the music. I love the kids' concerts, the candles at church, and the focus on Jesus. I don't even mind the shopping, or even the long drive home to be with family.

What I don't love is the crunch. Our everyday lives are fairly full, and we rely heavily on good routines and rhythms to keep us on track. Christmas, with extra festivities and responsibilities, can be hard on a schedule. (And, for that matter, on a budget!)

When we're racing the kids to church pageant practice, and then to pick out a Christmas tree, and then to the store to pick up groceries, and then home to do homework, we start to feel like there isn't enough—not enough time, not enough money, not enough patience.

That feeling of not enough can make me start to panic. How on earth are we going to get all this done in that amount of time? I begin snapping at those around me: "Hurry up!" "We don't have time for that!" "Didn't you get that done?" To my family, it can look like I hate Christmas.

It's ironic, isn't it? Because if there's one thing Christians are promised in lavish, unending abundance, it's time (John 3:16). We'll literally have forever to worship the Lord, to remember his goodness and salvation, and to celebrate with those we love. I don't know what life will be like in the new creation, but I don't think we'll be lamenting the tasks we didn't get done back in this life.

Remembering eternity awaits helps me relax today. If we don't get the perfect gifts ordered, or decorate the tree the day after Thanksgiving, or make it to every performance, that's OK. There will be plenty of time later.

The truth can also help us prioritize. If there is ample time *later*, what is important to do *now*? Since we have limited time on this broken planet, maybe we'd be better off using it to encourage a harried store clerk or say a prayer with a lonely neighbor. Maybe we could schedule coffee with an old friend or volunteer to help at church.

Maybe we could shift focus from not having enough time for *ourselves*, to seeing opportunities to share Christ with *others*.

While we do, we can trust that God, who created both time and tasks, sees what we need and will provide it (Matt. 6:25–34). We can trust his Spirit to help and guide us (John 14:26). And we can trust his peace, which surpasses all understanding, will guard both our hearts and our minds in Christ Jesus (Phil. 4:7).

RESPOND

What "not enough" makes you feel anxious this time of year? Not enough time? Money? Relationships? Given both our abundance and limitation, what deserves prioritization?

REJOICE

And ye, beneath life's crushing load,
Whose forms are bending low,
Who toil along the climbing way
With painful steps and slow,
Look now! for glad and golden hours
come swiftly on the wing.
O rest beside the weary road,
And hear the angels sing!
For lo!, the days are hastening on,
By prophet bards foretold,
When with the ever-circling years
Comes round the age of gold
When peace shall over all the earth
Its ancient splendors fling,
And the whole world give back the song
Which now the angels sing.

–Edmund Sears, "It Came Upon a Midnight Clear"

And the shepherds returned, glorifying and praising
God for all they had heard and seen, as it had
been told them.

LUKE 2:20

And the ransomed of the Lord shall return
and come to Zion with singing;
everlasting joy shall be upon their heads;
they shall obtain gladness and joy,
and sorrow and sighing shall flee away.

ISAIAH 35:10

JOY

Shepherd Candle

DAY 11

SURPRISED
BY JOY

Ivan Mesa

READ

"And the ransomed of the LORD shall return and come to Zion with singing; everlasting joy shall be upon their heads; they shall obtain gladness and joy, and sorrow and sighing shall flee away." (Isa. 35:10)

REFLECT

Christmas isn't always a festive season. Whether it's the absence of loved ones, the heartache of broken relationships, the toll of chronic suffering, or the unending battle against sin, it's not uncommon to end the year on a weary and joyless note. What word does the Lord offer those of us who barely make it to the finish line? He promises everlasting joy.

Nestled between two chapters of judgment and invasion, Isaiah 35 is a chapter suffused with joy for God's weary people. Even as they're about to experience the pain and consequences of their disobedience and rebellion, God extends a promise: it will not always be this way.

God's people would "return to Zion," meaning, Israel would leave their exile in Babylon and come back to Jerusalem. Why? Because they had been "ransomed." In the days of Moses, God had redeemed them by the blood of the lamb, and by his mighty hand he secured their exodus from Egypt. In this passage, he promises to redeem them in a second exodus. Despite their sin, God hadn't given up on them. They were still his redeemed people (Isa. 35:9). Sighing would soon give way to singing, and sorrow give way to joy.

Something even greater than the return from exile is coming for each of us. Isaiah's joyous language can't be contained by the events of 538 BC (2 Chron. 36:22–23; Ezra 1:1–4). There's a deeper promise in these verses—a better hope and a glorious day that's still to come.

As Christians, we still endure "sorrow and sighing" (cf. Rom. 8; 2 Cor. 4–5). We dwell in earthly tents as we sojourn to our heavenly home. Because we know something better is coming, we endure our various trials with hope (Rom. 5:3). Yes, this life is a difficult journey, but a glorious eternity awaits. We're promised that a heavenly Zion will one day descend on us (Heb. 12:22) and "gladness and joy will overtake [us]" (Isa. 35:10, NIV).

Why is this better day coming? Because we've been ransomed with greater blood than the Passover lamb. The babe in the manger was the second Adam, born to take away the sins of the world. How often are we robbed of joy when we believe that God sent his Son to the cross to purchase our pardon, but foolishly fear he won't carry us home (cf. Rom. 8:32)?

Not only will we have everlasting joy, but sadness and sighing will depart forever. In *The Lord of the Rings*, Samwise Gamgee awakens with delight: "Gandalf! I thought you were dead! But then I thought I was dead! Is everything sad going to come untrue?"[1]

Yes. In Christ, everything sad will indeed come untrue (Rev. 21:4–5). One day, we will awaken with eternal delight—this is the hope of Christmas.

RESPOND

What earthly sorrows make you long for heaven even more? How can our future hope make a difference in your life today?

REJOICE

O Savior, Child of Mary, who felt our human woe,
O Savior, King of glory, who dost our weakness know;
Bring us at length we pray, to the bright courts of Heaven,
And to the endless day!

–Michael Praetorius (Tr. by Theodore Baker),
"Lo, How a Rose E'er Blooming"

1.   J. R. R. Tolkien, *The Lord of the Rings*, 50th anniversary ed. (New York: HarperCollins, 2004), 951.

NEWS FOR THE NATIONS

Matt Smethurst

READ

"And in the same region there were shepherds out in the field, keeping watch over their flock by night. And an angel of the Lord appeared to them, and the glory of the Lord shone around them, and they were filled with great fear. And the angel said to them, 'Fear not, for behold, I bring you good news of great joy that will be for all the people. For unto you is born this day in the city of David a Savior, who is Christ the Lord.'" (Luke 2:8-11)

REFLECT

These shepherds had never seen a distant town illumining the midnight sky. Electric lights were still 18 centuries away.

And they certainly had never seen fireworks. Every single evening, the darkness descended yet again to engulf them, to swallow them. No category existed in their minds for the dazzling display that lit up the sky—and their lives—that night.

No wonder they collapse in terror.

But instead of judgment, they hear words of assurance: "Fear not" (v. 10). Before we turn to the angel's explanation, we dare not take for granted that an explanation is offered at all. A holy God is not obligated to give us reasons to trust him. He has every right to tell us what to do—"Quit being scared," for instance—and leave it at that. Just because we desire a reason doesn't mean we deserve one.

But God is not just holy; he is also generous and kind. He gives us what we don't deserve, including manifold reasons to obey his commands and trust his heart.

So, against this backdrop of bleating sheep and blinding fear, the angel clarifies why the shepherds have no reason to shudder: "I bring you good news of great joy" (v. 10). It's as if he's saying, "Get up! You can breathe now. We've not come to judge you; we've come to unveil the most magnificent news you will ever hear."

And what is this news? "For unto you is born this day in the city of David a Savior, who is Christ the Lord" (v. 11).

Notice two things in these verses.

First, the news is good and the joy is great because it's for *all* the people. The King in the manger won't be stingy with his mercy; in fact, he's on a mission to rescue every kind of rebel. Most basically, this promise means Jews *and* Gentiles, and yet by extension it encompasses the greatest to the least—sovereigns and shepherds, billionaires and beggars, missionaries and murderers, the pious and the profane. If you know yourself to be morally and spiritually bankrupt, you are not incidental to this Savior's mission; you are central to it. He's not looking to draft better talent. He comes for obscure herdsmen on the outskirts of the empire, unseen by elites and yet deeply loved by God. No matter who you are or where you are, these glad tidings are for you.

Second, notice who is born to us: "a Savior, who is Christ the Lord." This is not flattering. We were so lost and addicted to sin that nothing less than a cosmic rescue operation could free us. Some persons desire to have Jesus as Savior without bothering to follow him as Lord. Perhaps that even describes you. *I hope he forgives my sin; I just don't want him to mess with my life*. But friend, that is to want the benefits of Good Friday without the obligations of Easter Sunday. Do you only want to be delivered from sin's guilt but not also sin's power? If so, then you may be religious, but you are not yet saved.

This good news, though, should bring great joy: unto you is born not just a Savior who can pardon but a King who can transform. Will you let him? Will you give him control? The good news of the gospel, after all, is so much better than "Follow your heart." For the child in the manger grew up and said, "Follow me." Don't miss out.

RESPOND

Which are you more prone to think: *I'm too bad, so my sin can't be forgiven*, or *I'm forgiven, so my sin isn't too bad*? Take some time to confess before the Lord, thanking him that his mercy in Christ fully covers all your sin. Also, prayerfully consider areas that you may be minimizing sin in your life. Ask the Lord to give you a renewed desire for joyful obedience and trust in God's power to change you.

REJOICE

Joyful, all ye nations rise,
Join the triumph of the skies;
With the angelic host proclaim:
"Christ is born in Bethlehem."
Hark! The herald angels sing,
"Glory to the newborn King!"

–Charles Wesley, "Hark! The Herald Angels Sing"

DAY 13

PLEASURES FOREVERMORE

Collin Hansen

READ

"You make known to me the path of life; in your presence there is fullness of joy; at your right hand are pleasures forevermore." (Ps. 16:11)

REFLECT

I'll tell you what I want for Christmas this year. The path of life. Would someone let me know when you find it? That would be great. Thanks! Maybe this year the secret will end up wrapped beneath my Christmas tree.

Christmas evokes so many nostalgic memories that I imagine the holiday can set me back on course in the path of life. Every Christmas I think, *This year will be different. I'll slow down, savor the moments, enjoy the sounds and sights and smells. I'll spend the time thanking God for how he led me in the last year and how he promises to guide me in the next.* And every year I stumble downstairs on Christmas morning and collapse in an exhausted heap—especially if I'm up late assembling toys and the kids wake up early.

When I'm straying amid especially busy times like the holidays, Psalm 16:11 helps draw me home. I wish the path of life was trouble-free and straightforward (Matt.7:14). Then it might be easier to find and follow. But in my more spiritually lucid moments, I remember Jesus himself is the path—"the way, the truth, and the life" (John 14:6). And following him isn't so much about knowing where I'm going but trusting him to guide me.

I don't know why I think it would be better to know what's around the bend on the path of life. On March 10, 2020, would it have helped me to know what the next year had in store? Probably the opposite would have been true. I would have been overwhelmed with worry and grief. And yet through those dark days Jesus never left me. Because he is the path of life, there is fullness of joy in his presence. And not even a global pandemic and its ongoing aftermath can steal that joy.

The Christmas season bombards us with promises of pleasure through receiving the perfect gift. *If I could just get that red bow on a new car, then life would be OK. If someone special gave me that ring or necklace, then I'd be loved.* But we all know better, once we turn off the TV. I know this Christmas will look much like the ones before. I'll eat too much food and gain too much weight. My kids won't love their presents as much as I thought they would. Anticipation will give way to disappointment at some point when nostalgia doesn't match reality.

Nothing, though, can take away the pleasures of Christ. He carried his cross to Golgotha so he could be the path to life. When he ascended to the right hand of the Father, you and I could enjoy pleasures forevermore. That's the only Christmas gift we could ever really need.

RESPOND

Do you associate following Jesus with pleasure? What about Jesus brings you particular joy?

REJOICE

Jesus, joy of man's desiring,
Holy wisdom, love most bright;
Drawn by Thee, our souls aspiring
Soar to uncreated light.

–Martin Janus, "Jesus, Joy of Man's Desiring"

DAY 14

SPLIT PERSONALITY

Sarah Eekhoff Zylstra

READ

"You have put more joy in my heart than they have when their grain and wine abound." (Ps. 4:7)

REFLECT

When I was younger, Christmas seemed to have a split personality.

Religious Christmas was deep and serious. It was weeks of waiting, candles in the dark, and four-stanza hymns. It was extra church services and listening to Luke 2 (again) before opening gifts. It frowned on things like commercialism, Santa Claus, and saying "Happy Holidays!"

Secular Christmas, on the other hand, was bright and glittery. It was lights, and parties, and kitchen countertops loaded with cookies and chocolate. It was snowmen with black hats and reindeers with red noses. It was cousins to play with and a mountain of presents under the tree—some from Santa.

It can almost make you wonder if Christians know how to have fun. Is Christianity just a bunch rules keeping you from the real pleasures of life? Don't buy too much. Don't believe in magic. Don't drink too much. Don't have sex with your boyfriend. Don't swear. Don't gamble.

But if you dig into this, even a little bit, the lie gives way. The lesser amusements we turn to for happiness—sex, alcohol, a perfectly clean house, a new car, a bigger bank balance—deliver a burst of bliss that quickly wanes. Secular Christmas, with its enthusiastic sparkles, dumps us into the cold gray of January.

Christian joy is much weightier, more durable. It comes from a clean conscience washed by Jesus's blood (1 John 1:7), from confidence in a future God controls (Prov. 19:21), and from knowing we cannot be separated from a God who is working everything for our good (Rom. 8:28, 38–39).

Christian joy is also fun. "You shall rejoice before the LORD your God seven days," says Leviticus 23:40. "Shout for joy!" exclaims Psalm 32:11. "Sing and rejoice, O daughter of Zion," the Lord declares in Zechariah 2:10.

For comparison, here's a quote from Ruhollah Khomeini, the grand ayatollah of Iran.

Allah did not create man so that he could have fun. The aim of creation was for mankind to be put to the test through hardship and prayer. An Islamic regime must be serious in every field. There are no jokes in Islam. There is no humor in Islam. There is no fun in Islam. There can be no fun and joy in whatever is serious. Islam does not allow swimming in the sea and is opposed to radio and tele-

vision serials. Islam, however, allows marksmanship, horseback riding and competition.[1]

Place that next to Isaiah 65:18: "But be glad and rejoice forever in that which I create; for behold, I create Jerusalem to be a joy, and her people to be a gladness." Or David dancing before the Lord with all his might (2 Sam. 6:14). Or the Israelites whose "mouths were filled with laughter, [their] tongues with songs of joy" (Ps. 126:2, NIV).

Our Creator is the One who invented jokes and belly laughs and parties. He gave us friendships, dance moves, and the ability to come up with a perfectly timed one-liner. Jesus's very first miracle wasn't to destroy the wicked or even to feed the hungry, but to add wine to a week-long wedding party. When he returns for us, the celebration is going to be even more magnificent (Rev. 19:6–9).

I used to think Christmas had a split personality, but it doesn't. In truth, religious Christmas includes both "Silent Night" by candlelight *and* the pile of gifts around the tree. It's both serving at the food pantry *and* platters of food at Grandma's house. It's both "Joy to the World" *and* "Jingle Bells."

In fact, the solemnity of Advent wreaths and Bible reading *add* to the joy of family celebrations, twinkling light displays, and penning Christmas cards. Out of the deep joy of being right with God springs laughter and lightness. A heart that rests secure in God is also best positioned to enjoy family events (even difficult ones), to sing loudly, to delight in the gifts others receive, and to savor homemade cookies fresh out of the oven.

The Lord has put more joy in our hearts than they have when grain and wine abound.

---

1. Peter Hussein, *Islam in Its Own Words* (Morrisville: Lulu Self Publishing, 2018), 16.

RESPOND

Which religious aspects of the holiday seem dull or tedious beside the shine of secular Christmas? How can you remind yourself that a heart filled with joy in the Lord produces the best laughter?

REJOICE

Angels we have heard on high
Sweetly singing o'er the plains
And the mountains in reply
Echoing their joyous strains
Gloria, in excelsis Deo
Gloria, in excelsis Deo

–James Chadwick (English paraphrase),
"Angels We Have Heard on High"

DAY 15

JOY IN GIVING

Melissa Kruger

READ

"Thanks be to God for his inexpressible gift!" (2 Cor. 9:15)

REFLECT

It's the season of gift giving. I love considering just the right gifts for neighbors, friends, and family. Each person's name under the tree is special to me in some way. The part of gift giving I enjoy has little to do with money and everything to do with expression. Each type of gift communicates something from the giver to the receiver:

A gift that fulfills a need says, "I notice and care about you."

A gift that's a complete surprise says, "I know what you need, even if you didn't know you needed it."

A gift that can be enjoyed for years to come says, "I want to bless you with future joy."

A gift that comes with personal sacrifice says, "I love you more than I love myself."

Even though I love gift giving, as I face the hustle and bustle of shopping and see the materialism abounding in our culture, I find myself questioning, "What does any of this have to do with Jesus?" Is the way we celebrate Christmas just an excuse to overspend, overindulge, and focus too much on earthly treasures? Should I run from the stores, remove the presents from the tree, and find other ways to celebrate?

As I discussed my internal struggle with my husband, he kindly reminded me that gift giving is not just a reflection of worldly materialism (although it can be), but it's also a reflection of our Creator, who delights to give gifts to his people. Our conversation prompted me to ponder anew the gift given in Bethlehem.

Truly special gifts usually involve preparation and waiting. From the exit of Eden, a promise of redemption and a hope were given. The divine whisper continued speaking through all the prophets: *Something special is coming.* Wait for it. Watch for it. Hope in it.

And then, at just the right moment in time, God sent angels and a star in the heavens to declare: "The gift is here." Glory wrapped in flesh made his dwelling among us in the form of a baby.

It was unexpected. It was surprising. It was exactly what we needed.

The second Adam, born of a virgin, born far from the paradise of Eden, came and lived a sinless life. He resisted temptation. He wept. He rejoiced. He went to weddings. He made intimate friendships. He experienced betrayal. He healed. He taught. He loved. He lived a perfect life and died a sacrificial death. His people wanted an earthly kingdom, but he ushered in a heavenly one.

All of it was part of the gift.

When I consider all the reasons I love giving and receiving gifts, I realize that in Christ, God fulfills them all. In Jesus, God communicates:

I knew what you needed, even when you didn't know you needed it. (Rom. 5:15-19)

You are fully known and fully loved by me. (1 Cor. 13:1-12)

I want to give you future joy. (Rev. 21:1-4)

I love you more than I love myself. (John 15:13)

Christ is the one gift needed. He never wears out or loses shape. Like a treasure chest, deeply laden with all sorts of riches, new delights await, ready to be uncovered.

RESPOND

Consider this past year. How has your faith in Jesus given you joy? When you think of Jesus, what are you thankful for?

REJOICE

No more let sins and sorrows grow,
Nor thorns infest the ground;
He comes to make his blessings flow
Far as the curse is found,
Far as the curse is found,
Far as, far as, the curse is found.

-Isaac Watts, "Joy to the World"

And suddenly there was with the angel a multitude
of the heavenly host praising God and saying, "Glory
to God in the highest, and on earth peace among
those with whom he is pleased!"

LUKE 2:13–14

For God so loved the world, that he gave his only
Son, that whoever believes in him should not perish
but have eternal life.

JOHN 3:16

LOVE

Angel Candle

DAY 16

THE FATHER'S LOVE

Samuel James

READ

"For God so loved the world, that he gave his only Son, that whoever believes in him should not perish but have eternal life." (John 3:16)

REFLECT

Early in the morning, I wake and quietly make my way to the gray wing chair in my home office. I'm determined to be productive in these precious predawn hours. Only a few minutes into my routine, however, the door next to me slowly opens and my 4-year-old son walks in, bleary-eyed. All he wants to do is crawl into my lap and put a tired head on my shoulder. My plans for this moment are spoiled, but I couldn't care less.

Why? Because I'm this boy's father, and he's my son, and that is enough to make me welcome his intrusion with joy.

One of the reasons we miss drinking more deeply of God's love is that we forget to think of him as Father. We may know it's true because we've read our Bibles, but our intuitions still imagine God as a more distant figure. This isn't merely a shortcoming in our thinking; it's a tragic distortion of our view of God.

"Father" isn't a random nickname for God. It's who God fundamentally is. He *is* Father. God the Father has eternally begotten God the Son. Jesus taught us to pray, "Our Father." Why? Theologian Michael Reeves puts it like this: "This is who God has revealed himself to be: not first and foremost Creator or Ruler, but Father."[1]

Not all of us have fathers who loved and protected us. For many the word "father" is a pain, not a comfort. God sees this pain. He is the perfect Father, the One our hearts were made to know.

Understanding the perfect, fatherly character of God awakens the love of God in us. Jesus reminded us: if even sinful human fathers can genuinely love their children, our heavenly Father is infinitely more eager to shower unfathomable riches of love on us (Matt. 7:11). We're not tolerated employees or hired hands, but adopted sons of the Father (Rom. 8:15). God's love for his people isn't something he was manipulated or forced into feeling. God the Father, in his perfect, insurmountable fatherly compassion, sent his only begotten Son to the world to die, so that dying spiritual orphans, enslaved to sin, could become his children and hear their Father singing over them (Zeph. 3:17). Savor your position in the household of God—he delights in you, he loves you, and he welcomes you into his presence.

1.   Michael Reeves, *Delighting in the Trinity: An Introduction to the Christian Faith* (Downers Grove: IVP, 2012), 21.

When we look at the Christmas manger, we need to see more than a baby. We need to see a heavenly Father, the One who gave his only Son to us so we might become adopted sons and daughters. Could a Father this good, who gave this much, be anything but perfect for our weary, sinful, broken hearts?

RESPOND

How does knowing God as Father change how you feel toward him? How does it change what you think he feels toward you?

REJOICE

Of the Father's love begotten,
Ere the worlds began to be,
He is Alpha and Omega,
He the source, the ending he,
Of the things that are and have been,
And that future years shall see,
Evermore and evermore.

–Prudentius (Tr. by J. M. Neale), "Of the Father's Love Begotten"

DAY 17

TIME-SHIFTING LOVE

Brett McCracken

READ

"But when the fullness of time had come, God sent forth his Son, born of woman, born under the law, to redeem those who were under the law, so that we might receive adoption as sons. And because you are sons, God has sent the Spirit of his Son into our hearts, crying, 'Abba! Father!' So you are no longer a slave, but a son, and if a son, then an heir through God." (Gal. 4:4–7)

REFLECT

I mark time in my life based on when I met my wife, Kira. The first 27 years are the "pre-Kira" years—many of which were years of longing and waiting and wondering about the wife

I hoped I'd one day have. The last 11 years are the "post-Kira" years—in which my relationship with her has shaped me and altered my life's trajectory in all sorts of wonderful ways. What changed in that hinge point of my personal history? What signaled a dramatic shift in the two halves of my life? The arrival of love: the initiation of a new union, a new covenant, a new family.

The arrival of Jesus in history also marks a hinge point. We literally divide time according to his arrival: BC before Christ's birth, AD (anno Domini) after. History shifted course in dramatic fashion "when the fullness of time had come" (v. 4) and God sent forth his Son.

I've always loved the mysterious, lyrical phrase from today's reading: "when the fullness of time had come." How intriguing! Something about this particular point in time—the geopolitical dynamics of the Roman empire, the technological advances, the placement in Israel's history—made it the "fullness of time" moment when the temporal needed to be punctured by the eternal and forever changed. And, like the "fullness of time" moment in my own life, the breaking and restarting of time had to do with the entrance of a love that changed everything.

Sometimes I stop to reflect with deep gratitude on the arrival of Kira into my life, and the way our love in marriage has produced new life (both spiritually, in terms of our growth, and physically, in the form of children!). How much more miraculous, then, is the arrival of Jesus into the world—the moment when humans were given hope for new life, through covenant union with him. He came not only to free us from sin but to invite us into his family. His arrival made it possible for slaves to become sons, debtors to become heirs, the lonely to be placed in family. His birth, death, and resurrection showed the world a love it had never seen before, and invited alienated sinners into a Spirit-formed community marked by a love that would never fail (1 Cor. 13:8).

Everything truly did change because of Jesus's arrival on the scene of history. It's no wonder time restarted. It's no wonder Christmas is the world's most festive holiday. Or maybe it *is* a wonder—a magnificent and miraculous true story we should never tire of telling.

RESPOND

Reflect on the time-shifting arrival of love in the form of Jesus. Think about what the BC world was like before him, and what we now have in the AD time after his appearing. Pray and give thanks to God for the love, freedom, and rest we can now experience because of his Son.

REJOICE

Come, thou long expected Jesus
Born to set thy people free
From our fears and sins release us
Let us find our rest in thee

–Charles Wesley, "Come, Thou Long Expected Jesus"

DAY 18

GOD IS LOVE

Quina Aragon

READ

"But God, being rich in mercy, because of the great love with which he loved us, even when we were dead in our trespasses, made us alive together with Christ." (Eph. 2:4–5)

REFLECT

In the dark void of eternity past, there was God, eternally existing as Father, Son, and Spirit. The apostle John tells us, "God is love" (1 John 4:8, 16) so it's safe to say love preexisted creation. Our Creator—even before he could be called Creator—has always existed in a unified community of love. The Father has always poured out delight in his Son, who is "the radiance of the glory of God and the exact imprint of his nature" (Heb. 1:3). Love has forever flowed between the Father, Son, and Holy Spirit.

But love, by nature, spreads. It moves outward. When God said, "Let there be light," it was his Word—his own Son—that accomplished the task (Gen. 1:3; cf. John 1:1–3). The love the Father has always had for his Son, in a sense, spilled over to make creation. By his great love, God made us in his image—his representatives sent to proclaim his glory and worth all over the world.

You know what happened, though. Our greatest-grand-parents, Adam and Eve, turned against the loving heart of God. And since then, we're all born, as our passage says, "dead in our trespasses"—dark as the pretemporal void and ripe for God's judgment.

"But God" (that glorious phrase!) is rich in mercy. His rivers of kindness never run dry. This God, who *is* love, spoke again. He sent to us his Word, clothed in flesh—Jesus Christ. Jesus, the Son of God, showed us the very heart of the Father: he loves sinners. He loves you and me. Christ died in our place as the wrath-soaking substitute to make us beloved children of God.

But God spoke yet again. He called you—you who were dead in your sins—by the power of his Spirit to become alive with Christ. He said again, to you directly this time: "Let there be light!" (cf. 2 Cor. 4:6). Why would God pursue a rebel like you or like me? Why would the hero die for the villain? It's "because of the great love with which he loved us" (v. 4).

Just as God's Trinitarian love spilled over to make creation, so his Trinitarian love burst forth to re-create a fallen humanity. Our God, dear friends, is love. And he's got the resume—scars and all—to prove it.

RESPOND

Do you find it hard to believe God loves you (as in, you specifically)? How does the fact that God is love give you confidence in his loving care for you today?

REJOICE

Divinely free his mercy flows,
Forgives my sins, allays my woes;
And bids approaching death remove,
And crowns me with a father's love.

–Anne Steele, "Awake, My Soul, Awake"

FROM SPLENDOR TO SQUALOR

Matt Smethurst

READ

"Have this mind among yourselves, which is yours in Christ Jesus, who, though he was in the form of God, did not count equality with God a thing to be grasped, but emptied himself, by taking the form of a servant, being born in the likeness of men. And being found in human form, he humbled himself by becoming obedient to the point of death, even death on a cross. Therefore God has highly exalted him and bestowed on him the name that is above every name, so that at the name of Jesus every knee should bow, in heaven and on earth and under the earth, and every tongue confess that Jesus Christ is Lord, to the glory of God the Father." (Phil. 2:5–11)

REFLECT

Many religions throughout history have acknowledged the value of humility. None has dared speak of a humble God. The reason is simple: the notion of *humility* applied to *deity* is seen as a category mistake. So the claim that the biblical God—not a member of a pantheon, not an option on a menu of deities, but the one Creator of all—that *he* would stoop to serve his creatures, all the way down to a torturous cross, is not just startling. It's scandalous.

But that's precisely what happened. This passage resounds with the news that even though God the Son had it all—the worship of angels, the infinite love of Father and Spirit—he still came from the splendor of heaven to the squalor of a stable. And on a lonely night in a little town called Bethlehem, he began a journey of obedience to his Father—a journey that would culminate 33 years later on a hill outside Jerusalem, where he suffered on a cross for rebels like us. And what compelled him? *Indescribable love.* Indeed, "greater love has no one than this, that someone lay down his life for his friends" (John 15:13). There is no more perfect example of self-giving love than the One who left heaven when he could have stayed, and who stayed on the cross when he could have left.[1]

But Christ's humiliation is not the end of the story. In Philippians 2:9, Paul broadcasts the reward: "Therefore God has highly exalted him." This phrase is shorthand for the whole complex of events—resurrection, ascension, coronation, heavenly reign—subsequent to his sin-bearing death.

And one day soon, everybody in the universe will bow before this King of glory. There are only two options: you can

---

1.   Some of the material in this section is adapted from Matt Smethurst, *Deacons: How They Serve and Strengthen the Church* (Wheaton: Crossway, 2021), 126–27.

either bow to him now as Savior, or bow to him later as Judge. But every knee, including yours, will bow.

Friend, do not let another Christmas go by without staring—really staring—at the depths to which your Savior plunged himself in order to raise you up and seat you with him in the heavenly places (Eph. 2:6).

RESPOND

This passage doesn't just move us to marvel at Jesus's one-way love—it also calls us to cultivate his mindset (v. 5). Before this year is over, who is someone in your life you could stoop to serve? How and when could you do it? Few things will better spark encouragement, and perhaps gospel witness, than a deliberate act of self-giving love.

REJOICE

From the squalor of a borrowed stable,
By the Spirit and a virgin's faith;
To the anguish and the shame of scandal,
Came the Savior of the human race.

–Stuart Townend, "Immanuel"

WHAT LOVE FEELS LIKE

Betsy Childs Howard

READ

"This is how God showed his love among us: He sent his one and only Son into the world that we might live through him." (1 John 4:9, NIV)

REFLECT

Fear. Abandonment. Shame. Surely Mary felt these emotions as she and her betrothed, far from home, looked for a place to stay. Every time a door closed and they were turned away, the situation seemed more desperate. Did she know she was ready to deliver when they made their bed in the stable, or did the realization come upon her suddenly in the night?

Straw needling her back. Sweat behind her neck. Nausea. Labor pains. These are just a few sensations Mary may have felt in the lead-up to the first Christmas. Childbirth is wonderful, but nothing about it is comfortable.

On our hardest days, it's not easy to feel God's love. We may feel pain, doubt, confusion, or despair because we cannot understand what God is doing. When our circumstances get worse instead of better, we may question whether God loves us.

I don't know if Mary questioned God that night in Bethlehem as she pushed through contractions, but I do know she was experiencing God's love in a way exponentially deeper than anything that could ever be felt. She was giving birth to the Savior who would save her from her sins. What did that experience feel like? It felt like pain.

The Bible is full of stories of believers who looked like they had been forgotten by God when in reality, they were living through a crucial part of his salvation plan. Consider the stories of Joseph, Hannah, David, Daniel, Esther, and Elijah, just for a start. The very circumstances that might have made them feel abandoned by God were orchestrated by him to show his covenant-keeping love to the people of Israel.

We expect love to feel warm, comforting, and reassuring . . . and one day it will. As Mary gave birth to Jesus, she was feeling the labor pains that came into the world through the curse of sin (Gen. 3:16). But the baby she bore would reverse the curse so that one day there will be no more tears of pain.

When we feel pain, sorrow, bewilderment, or helplessness, we haven't been forgotten by God. God's love for you is not based on your feelings or your circumstances. It's based on his unchanging character, which is always good. The evidence of that love is the gift of his beloved Son—the baby Mary cradled in her arms.

RESPOND

How have you seen God's love in your life recently? Think beyond the obvious blessings to the experiences that have shown you the tangible love of God in your life.

REJOICE

Love came down at Christmas,
Love all lovely, Love Divine,
Love was born at Christmas,
Star and Angels gave the sign.

–Christina Rossetti, "Love Came Down at Christmas"

The next day he saw Jesus coming toward him, and said, "Behold, the Lamb of God, who takes away the sin of the world!"

JOHN 1:29

For by grace you have been saved through faith. And this is not your own doing; it is the gift of God, not a result of works, so that no one may boast. For we are his workmanship, created in Christ Jesus for good works, which God prepared beforehand, that we should walk in them.

EPHESIANS 2:8–10

FAITH

Christ Candle

BLESSED ARE THOSE WHO HAVE NOT SEEN

Megan Hill

READ

"Jesus said to him, 'Have you believed because you have seen me? Blessed are those who have not seen and yet have believed.'" (John 20:29)

REFLECT

The Advent story is filled with people who got to see Jesus face-to-face. Mary and Joseph, of course, were the first to set eyes on God in human flesh, to hold his hands, to kiss his feet. They were quickly joined by others. The shepherds arrived next: "Let us go over to Bethlehem and see," they told one another (Luke 2:15). Simeon also saw the child—even held him in his arms (Luke 2:28). Anna saw him (Luke 2:36–38). The wise men saw him (Matt. 2:10–11). And those initial visitors were just a small fraction of the multitudes who would soon come to sit at the incarnate Savior's feet.

I confess to feeling a little jealous.

I'd like to see Jesus too. I'd like to gaze on his face—to learn the contour of his chin and the color of his eyes. I'd like to hear his voice with physical ears. I'd like to touch his hands and worship at his feet. Thankfully, today's verse speaks to everyone born too late to be at either the manger or the tomb. We haven't seen our Savior face-to-face. But Jesus says we are blessed.

We are those of whom Peter says, "though you have not seen him, you love him" (1 Pet. 1:8) and who Paul says, "walk by faith, not by sight" (2 Cor. 5:7). While the crowds in Jesus's earthly lifetime often sought him for the dazzle of a miracle or the spectacle of a sign, we seek our unseen Savior by faith—a faith that could only come from his Spirit. If we have not seen and yet still believe, we can have confidence that he lives with us and is at work in us (cf. John 14:17). Truly, we are blessed.

The manger is empty, and the tomb is empty too. Ultimately, it would be foolish to look for Christ in either of those places. Instead, we turn the eyes of faith heavenward, "[seeking] the things that are above, where Christ is, seated at the right hand of God" (Col. 3:1). Do we want to see Jesus? We must seek him where he is. We approach him in worship, we seek him in prayer, and we gaze on him in his Word.

We may not have made it to Bethlehem on that starry night, but Christ is nevertheless present with us by his Word and Spirit—particularly in the gathering of his church. We may not have touched his swaddling cloths or heard his newborn cries, but we have everything we need to experience him. His sensible signs are bread and wine, his voice resounds from a pulpit and a page, his eyes and ears and hands are on display in the weekly assembly of his beloved body.

And one day, just as he ascended, he will return. Writing from his lonely exile on Patmos, John encourages our hearts: "Behold, he is coming with the clouds, and every eye will see him" (Rev. 1:7).

"Amen. Come, Lord Jesus!" (Rev. 22:20).

RESPOND

Would you like to see Jesus? In what ways is walking by faith a blessing? How do you experience Christ by faith?

REJOICE

Not in that poor lowly stable, with the oxen standing by,
We shall see him, but in heaven, set at God's right hand on high;
When like stars his children crowned all in white
shall wait around.

–Cecil Frances Alexander, "Once in Royal David's City"

THE BLESSING OF BELIEVING

Betsy Childs Howard

READ

"Blessed is she who has believed that the Lord would fulfill his promises to her!" (Luke 1:45, NIV)

REFLECT

When Gabriel told Mary she would conceive a son who would reign on David's throne, she (understandably) asked, "How will this be, since I am a virgin?" (Luke 1:34).

When the angel replied that the Holy Spirit would come upon her and the power of the Most High would overshadow her so that her child would be the Son of God (Luke 1:35), this answered Mary's question—she now knew she would not conceive in the ordinary way—but it raised a thousand others. Two millennia later, we are no closer to understanding the biology of the incarnation than Mary was that day in Nazareth!

How Christ's conception and birth would take place weren't the only unknowns for Mary. Surely her betrothed would abandon her when her pregnancy was discovered. How would she live and support her baby? How would an impoverished boy from Nazareth rise to reign on David's throne?

Mary didn't let all the unknowns prevent her from trusting the word the angel spoke to her that day. She didn't have to understand to believe. Hebrews 11:1 tells us that faith is the "assurance of things hoped for, the conviction of things not seen." Mary didn't have to see in her mind's eye how God could work out his promises to believe that he would.

It's easier to believe God's promises when you think you understand how God is going to work them out. But when we can't fathom how God will do something, we can believe it by faith. We can believe God will supply all our needs (Phil. 4:19) without having any idea how he's going to meet our specific needs. We can believe God will help us endure and escape from temptation (1 Cor. 10:13) without knowing what the way of escape will be. We can believe one day God will bring full and complete justice (Ps. 37) even though we see the same injustices persist year after year.

God knows the answers to all our questions, just as he knew the answers to Mary's. He knew the Son of God would become man. That Joseph would be commanded in a dream to take Mary as his wife. That Mary's son would grow in wisdom and stature and favor with God and man. He knew Jesus would break the power of sin and death, not by military might but by laying down his life for us and rising again to reign eternally. And he knows exactly how he will fulfill every promise he has made to you.

RESPOND

What promises has God made that you find hard to believe? Are you willing to believe them by faith, even if you don't understand how God's going to fulfill them?

REJOICE

How silently, how silently, the wondrous gift is giv'n!
So God imparts to human hearts the blessings of his heaven.
No ear may hear his his coming, but in this world of sin,
Where meek souls will receive him still, the dear Christ enters in.

–Phillips Brooks, "O Little Town of Bethlehem"

DAY 23

THE CHOICE

Brett McCracken

READ

"Then Pilate said to him, 'So you are a king?' Jesus answered, 'You say that I am a king. For this purpose I was born and for this purpose I have come into the world—to bear witness to the truth. Everyone who is of the truth listens to my voice.'" (John 18:37)

REFLECT

It can be tempting at Christmastime—as we reflect on baby Jesus and the serene imagery of him cradled in Mary's arms, wrapped in swaddling clothes—to downplay or forget his supreme kingly authority. Jesus is God made flesh, the King of kings, the authority before which everything will bow, and compared to which every other authority pales. Our response to Jesus is not just about admiration or appreciation.

It demands allegiance. We must enthrone him in our hearts and submit to his reign. If we don't, he's just a holiday symbol as pleasant-yet-powerless as poinsettias and Christmas trees.

Advent presents everyone with a clear choice: bow down and worship the Christ, recognizing his authoritative claim on every square inch of the universe, *or* simply shrug at nativity niceties, drink some eggnog, and live your life as you see fit. There is no middle ground. Jesus is either the real, reigning king of your life, or he's a fiction as fantastical as Santa Claus.

What, you might ask, is the nature of Jesus's authority to occupy this "King of kings" role? Pilate wondered the same thing. Certainly, Jesus's authority looks different than what we're used to in a king or ruler. His authority is not found in worldly riches, military power, or political prowess. His authority comes from his association with God's truth. "I was born and for this purpose I have come into the world," he says, "to bear witness to the truth" (John 18:37). Elsewhere he says he is "the way, the truth, and the life" (John 14:6), and that those who follow his words will "know the truth, and the truth will set you free" (John 8:32). John starts his Gospel on this note, describing Jesus as eternal, ever-existing truth that takes on flesh (John 1:1–18).

But a lot of people claim to speak the truth, you might argue. How do we know which person's "truth" claim is actually true? Why believe Jesus when he talks about himself as *the* truth? That question brings us back to the choice before us: either believe Jesus is who he says he is—and thus bow down before him—or don't, and go on our merry way.

Jesus makes it clear what's at stake in the choice. "Everyone who is of the truth listens to my voice," he says. If we want to be on the side of truth, we'll listen to Jesus. We'll acknowledge him as King. If we look to any other foundation, or bow to any other king, we'll be on shaky ground, forever wandering and captive to fluid feelings, ephemeral trends, and whatever regime makes the rules in the moment.

Jesus offers truth that sets us free—truth to build a life on. But we can't follow him *partially* or listen to his words *selectively*. We must either enthrone him fully in our hearts, living in light of his lordship, or reject him completely. That's the choice.

RESPOND

Are you living "all in" in response to the kingship of Christ? Reflect on aspects of your life you haven't submitted to the lordship of Jesus. Is there something you want to keep under *your* control? With the help of the Spirit, how can you choose today to bring all of yourself to Christ in worship and allegiance?

REJOICE

So bring him incense, gold, and myrrh
Come, peasant, king, to own him
The King of kings salvation brings
Let loving hearts enthrone him

–William Chatterton Dix, "What Child Is This?"

DAY 24

WHO IS THE OBJECT OF YOUR FAITH?

Melissa Kruger

READ

"And Jesus answered them, 'Have faith in God.'" (Mark 11:22)

REFLECT

It's that time of year again. Decorative signs, advertisements, and commercials encourage us with the familiar messages:

"Just Believe"

"Have Faith"

"A Season of Hope"

At first glance these tidings may warm our hearts as we go about our way, humming Christmas music as we shop.

Yet, as I stop to reflect upon these phrases, I wonder, *What exactly do they mean?* Each of these statements is missing an essential element—the object of one's belief, faith, or hope.

One could read these messages and easily interpret that we are to "Just believe in Santa," or "Have faith in the goodness of mankind," or that this is "A season of hope" because we are looking forward to lovely times with families or gifts around the tree.

Understood in this way, these messages fall flat and bring little encouragement. Believing in Santa can be somewhat unsettling when you consider the song we sing about him:

He sees you when you're sleeping

He knows when you're awake

He knows if you've been bad or good

So be good for goodness' sake!

It's sobering to consider a large, bearded man dressed all in red velvet and smoking a pipe, keeping watch over us to see whether we've been good enough. Such a Jolly Old Elf's works-based righteousness might be more cause for fear and trembling than happiness and joy.

The same is true as we consider placing our faith in mankind or hoping in family gatherings. As we look around our world, hostility, racism, greed, discord, and disease dominate the news. We are a human race plagued with many struggles, and often these show up in our own families. And it's not just the world "out there," but also the person I look at in the mirror that causes me to pause before placing my faith in mankind or hoping in perfect family gatherings.

These familiar Christmas phrases are problematic because they are incomplete. It's not enough to simply be a hopeful person or be full of faith. It's essential for us to consider exactly where we are placing our belief, faith, and hope. The object of our faith is the essential substance of it. When we lose sight of the actual meaning of our faith, then we lose the very thing that sustains it.

The joy of the Christmas message is so much richer, deeper, and more beautiful than any other story that's ever been told. Glory was wrapped in flesh and dwelt among us, so that we could be wrapped in righteousness and dwell with God. Jesus lived a perfect life so he could be the perfect sacrifice for all that is wrong both in our own lives and in the world.

Without Jesus our belief has no merit, our faith has no basis, and our hope has no anchor. *In Jesus*, we find the joy of believing. *In Jesus*, we know this to be a season of hope. *In Jesus*, we find the substance of our faith.

RESPOND

What person or thing are you tempted to trust in for your joy? What would it look like today for you to put your faith and trust fully in Jesus to provide for all your needs?

REJOICE

God rest ye merry, gentlemen
Let nothing you dismay
Remember Christ our Savior
Was born on Christmas Day
To save us all from Satan's pow'r
When we were gone astray
Oh tidings of comfort and joy
Comfort and joy
Oh tidings of comfort and joy

–Author unknown, "God Rest Ye Merry, Gentlemen"

DAY 25

BORN TO DIE

Collin Hansen

READ

"But now the righteousness of God has been manifested apart from the law, although the Law and the Prophets bear witness to it—the righteousness of God through faith in Jesus Christ for all who believe. For there is no distinction: for all have sinned and fall short of the glory of God, and are justified by his grace as a gift, through the redemption that is in Christ Jesus, whom God put forward as a propitiation by his blood, to be received by faith. This was to show God's righteousness, because in his divine forbearance he had passed over former sins. It was to show his righteousness at the present time, so that he might be just and the justifier of the one who has faith in Jesus." (Rom. 3:21–26)

REFLECT

Why did Jesus come to dwell among us? You know he didn't need to make the effort. He could have left us to our sin, and he would have been just to condemn us. All of us have sinned and fallen short of the glory of God our Creator. If he only came to teach us some moral truths, he didn't need to go to the cross. The law had already revealed the character of God in all his awesome holiness, and righteousness, and goodness.

So why did he come? He came to fulfill the law by living in perfect obedience to his Father and complete love for everyone else he met. He came to walk in faith where Israel had failed. He came to teach us the meaning of his life—and his death. He was born to die so we who believe would live forever.

With the birth of Jesus on that holy night came the dawn of redeeming grace. Don't skip over that word "redeeming." What does it mean to be redeemed? It means we've been purchased for a price. We carried a debt to sin because we rebelled against God's law. And Jesus set us free. He redeemed us. But how? In the only way he could, so that God could be just and the justifier at the same time. Jesus offered himself as the substitutionary sacrifice for our sin. He died the death we deserved so that God the just would be satisfied.

What's left for us to do? To receive the greatest gift of all—justification. Jesus takes on our sin, and we get his righteousness. And how do we claim this gift? By faith. You won't find a better deal. But it's only available to the humble. To the desperate. To everyone who realizes they have no other options. This gift doesn't belong to anyone who thinks they deserve it.

The justified realize God would have been just to punish them. They know their best efforts to keep the law would have fallen far short. It's as if the biggest Christmas gifts belonged to the children who knew they deserved coal in their stocking. Jesus is the anti-Santa. He knows we belong on the naughty list. And that's why he came to save us. That's why he set aside the glories of heaven for the womb of his mother Mary. He was born to die. Even better, after he was delivered up for our trespasses, he was raised to life for our justification (Rom. 4:25).

Make sure you claim that gift this Christmas. Come in faith and leave justified.

RESPOND

How can God be both just and justifier at the same time? How does knowledge of your sin grow your grateful love to God?

REJOICE

Silent night, holy night
Son of God, love's pure light
Radiant beams from thy holy face
With the dawn of redeeming grace

–Joseph Mohr (Tr. by John Freeman Young), "Silent Night"

CONTRIBUTORS

QUINA ARAGON is an assistant editor and administrative assistant for women's initiatives for The Gospel Coalition. She's also an author and spoken-word artist residing in Tampa, Florida, with her husband, Jon, and daughter. Jon and Quina are members of Living Faith Bible Fellowship. Her first children's book, *Love Made*, poetically retells the story of creation through a Trinitarian lens of overflowing love. Its sequel, *Love Gave*, poetically retells the incarnation and good news of Jesus Christ through that same Trinitarian lens. You can find her at QuinaAragon.com.

WINFREE BRISLEY serves as an editor for The Gospel Coalition. She and her husband, Will, have three sons and live in Charlotte, North Carolina, where they are members of Uptown Church (PCA).

JUSTIN DILLEHAY is a pastor of Grace Baptist Church in Hartsville, Tennessee, where he resides with his wife, Tilly, and his children, Norah, Agnes, and Henry. He is a contributing editor of The Gospel Coalition.

COURTNEY DOCTOR serves as the coordinator of women's initiatives for The Gospel Coalition. She's the author of *From Garden to Glory: A Bible Study on the Bible's Story* and *Steadfast: A Devotional Bible Study on the Book of James*. Courtney and her husband, Craig, have four children, two daughters-in-law, and five amazing grandchildren.

COLLIN HANSEN serves as vice president for content and editor in chief of The Gospel Coalition. He has written and contributed to many books, most recently *Gospelbound: Living with Resolute Hope in an Anxious Age*, and hosts the *Gospelbound* podcast. He and his wife belong to Redeemer Community Church in Birmingham, Alabama, and he serves on the advisory board of Beeson Divinity School.

MEGAN HILL serves as an editor for The Gospel Coalition. She is the author of several books, including *A Place to Belong: Learning to Love the Local Church*. She lives with her husband and four children in Massachusetts, where they belong to West Springfield Covenant Community Church.

BETSY CHILDS HOWARD is an editor for The Gospel Coalition. She is the author of *Seasons of Waiting: Walking by Faith When Dreams Are Delayed* and the children's book *Arlo and the Great Big Cover-Up*. In 2017 her husband, Bernard, planted Good Shepherd Anglican Church in Manhattan, where they live with their son.

SAMUEL JAMES is an associate acquisitions editor at Crossway Books and editor of Letter & Liturgy.

MELISSA KRUGER serves as the director of women's initiatives for The Gospel Coalition. She's the author of multiple books, including *The Envy of Eve: Finding Contentment in a Covetous World*, *Walking with God in the Season of Motherhood*, and *Growing Together: Taking Mentoring Beyond Small Talk and*

Prayer Requests. Her husband, Mike, is the president of Reformed Theological Seminary and they have three children.

BRETT MCCRACKEN is a senior editor and director of communications at The Gospel Coalition. He is the author of several books, including *The Wisdom Pyramid: Feeding Your Soul in a Post-Truth World* and *Uncomfortable: The Awkward and Essential Challenge of Christian Community.* Brett and his wife, Kira, live in Santa Ana, California, with their two sons. They belong to Southlands Church, where Brett serves as an elder.

IVAN MESA is books editor for The Gospel Coalition. He's editor of *Before You Lose Your Faith: Deconstructing Doubt in the Church.* He and his wife, Sarah, have three children, and they live in eastern Georgia.

MATT SMETHURST is managing editor of The Gospel Coalition and author of *Deacons: How They Serve and Strengthen the Church* and *Before You Open Your Bible: Nine Heart Postures for Approaching God's Word.* He and his wife, Maghan, have three children and live in Richmond, Virginia. They are in the process of planting River City Baptist Church.

SARAH EEKHOFF ZYLSTRA is senior writer and faith-and-work editor for The Gospel Coalition. She is also the coauthor of *Gospelbound: Living with Resolute Hope in an Anxious Age.* She lives with her husband and two sons in the suburbs of Chicago, where they are active members of Orland Park Christian Reformed Church.

TGC THE GOSPEL COALITION

The Gospel Coalition (TGC) supports the church in making disciples of all nations, by providing gospel-centered resources that are trusted and timely, winsome and wise.

Guided by a Council of more than 40 pastors in the Reformed tradition, TGC seeks to advance gospel-centered ministry for the next generation by producing content (including articles, podcasts, videos, courses, and books) and convening leaders (including conferences, virtual events, training, and regional chapters).

In all of this we want to help Christians around the world better grasp the gospel of Jesus Christ and apply it to all of life in the 21st century. We want to offer biblical truth in an era of great confusion. We want to offer gospel-centered hope for the searching.

Join us by visiting TGC.org so you can be equipped to love God with all your heart, soul, mind, and strength, and to love your neighbor as yourself.